WALLINGFORD PUBLIC LIBRARY
WALLINGFORD, CONNECTICUT 06492

Geography Starts

FORESTS

Andy Owen
and
Miranda Ashwell

Heinemann Interactive Library
Des Plaines, Illinois

WALLINGFORD PUBLIC LIBRARY
WALLINGFORD, CONNECTICUT 06492

J 577.3
OWE

© 1998 Reed Educational & Professional Publishing
Published by Heinemann Interactive Library,
an imprint of Reed Educational & Professional Publishing,
1350 East Touhy Avenue, Suite 240 West
Des Plaines, IL 60018

All rights reserved. No part of this publication may be reproduced or transmitted in any form or by any means, electronic or mechanical, including photocopying, recording, taping, or any information storage and retrieval system, without permission in writing from the publisher.

Designed by Susan Clarke
Illustrations by Oxford Illustrators (maps pp.23, 25, 27) and Hardlines (pp.11, 18)
Printed in Hong Kong

02 01 00 99
10 9 8 7 6 5 4 3 2

Library of Congress Cataloging-in-Publication Data
Owen, Andy, 1961-
Forests / Andy Owen and Miranda Ashwell.
p. cm. — (Geography starts)
Includes bibliographical references and index.
Summary: Introduces the various forests of the world, including mangrove, broadleaf, evergreen, and rainforests.
ISBN 1-57572-610-6 (lib. bdg.)
1. Forests and forestry—Juvenile literature. 2. Trees—Juvenile literature. [1. Forests and forestry. 2. Trees.] I. Ashwell, Miranda, 1957- . II. Title. III. Series: Owen, Andy, 1961- Geography starts.
SD376.O84 1998
333.75—dc21 97-34418
CIP
AC

Acknowledgments
The Publishers would like to thank the following for permission to reproduce photographs: Andy Owen, p. 7; BBC/Jurgen Freund, p. 14; Geonex, pp. 22, 24, 26; Magnum/M.K. Nichols, p. 10; NHPA, p. 13 (Ken Griffiths), p. 15 (David Woodfall), p. 20 (John Shaw); Oxford Scientific Films, p. 4 (John Downer), p. 12 (Belinda Wright); Panos/Dominic Sansoni, p. 29; Robert Harding Picture Library/Simon Harris, p. 28; Still Pictures, p. 21 (William Campbell), pp. 16, 17 (Nigel Dickinson), p. 19 (Mark Edwards), p.5 (Pierre Gleizes); Telegraph Colour Library, pp.6, 8, 9.

Cover photograph: Robert Harding Picture Library

Our thanks to Betty Root for her comments in the preparation of this book.

Every effort has been made to contact copyright holders of any material reproduced in this book. Any omissions will be rectified in subsequent printings if notice is given to the publisher.

Some words are shown in bold, like this. You can find out what they mean by looking in the glossary.

BT 19.92 / 17.26 7/01

Contents

Trees and Forests

A forest is a large area of land covered by trees. Trees have been growing in this forest for hundreds of years. Wild plants grow under the trees.

This is a natural forest. People did not plant the trees.

Machines are used to cut the trees to the same shape and size.

These rows of trees were planted by people. The fruit is picked and sold.

Forests in Cold Places

Pine trees have special leaves called needles. The needles are long, hard, and thin. This protects them from the cold and snow.

Pine cones are the fruit of pine trees.

Pine trees have been planted on this steep hill.

Farmers cannot grow crops on steep hills. They plant pine trees instead. Wood from these trees is used to make paper, houses, and furniture.

Broadleaved Trees

an oak tree in winter

Broadleaved trees have wide leaves that fall off in autumn. The leaves rot into the soil and help other plants to grow.

the same oak tree in summer

New leaves grow when the weather gets warmer. Sunlight can still reach the plants growing under the tree.

Rainforests

Rainforests are very hot. It rains nearly every day. Many different plants and trees grow in a rainforest. Many kinds of birds and animals live in the trees.

Trees grow very tall in the rainforests.

The top of the trees is called the canopy. Leaves here get the most light.

It is much darker under the canopy.

Young plants grow fast to reach the light. Plants that don't get light will die.

The canopy traps the warm, damp air

the rainforest canopy

Forest Fires

Trees become dry and burn easily when there is no rain. Oils in the leaves make the fire very hot.

This forest fire in Australia spreads very quickly.

Some plants are helped by fire. The heat makes some seeds start to grow, and the ash makes the soil rich for them.

Some plants grow back quickly after a fire.

Mangrove Forests

Mangroves are trees that grow on the coasts of hot countries. Their roots protect the land from waves that might wash the mud away.

a young mangrove tree growing in the sea

Mangrove trees grow
in salty sea water.

Mangroves have special roots that grow in the air above the mud. The trees take in air through these roots.

Cutting Down Forests

Many trees must be cut down to build one road.

Some trees take hundreds of years to grow. It takes only minutes to cut down a tree.

Rainforests are cut down and their wood is sold around the world. The animals that live in the forests lose their homes.

Thousands of trees are cut down every day.

Washing Away the So

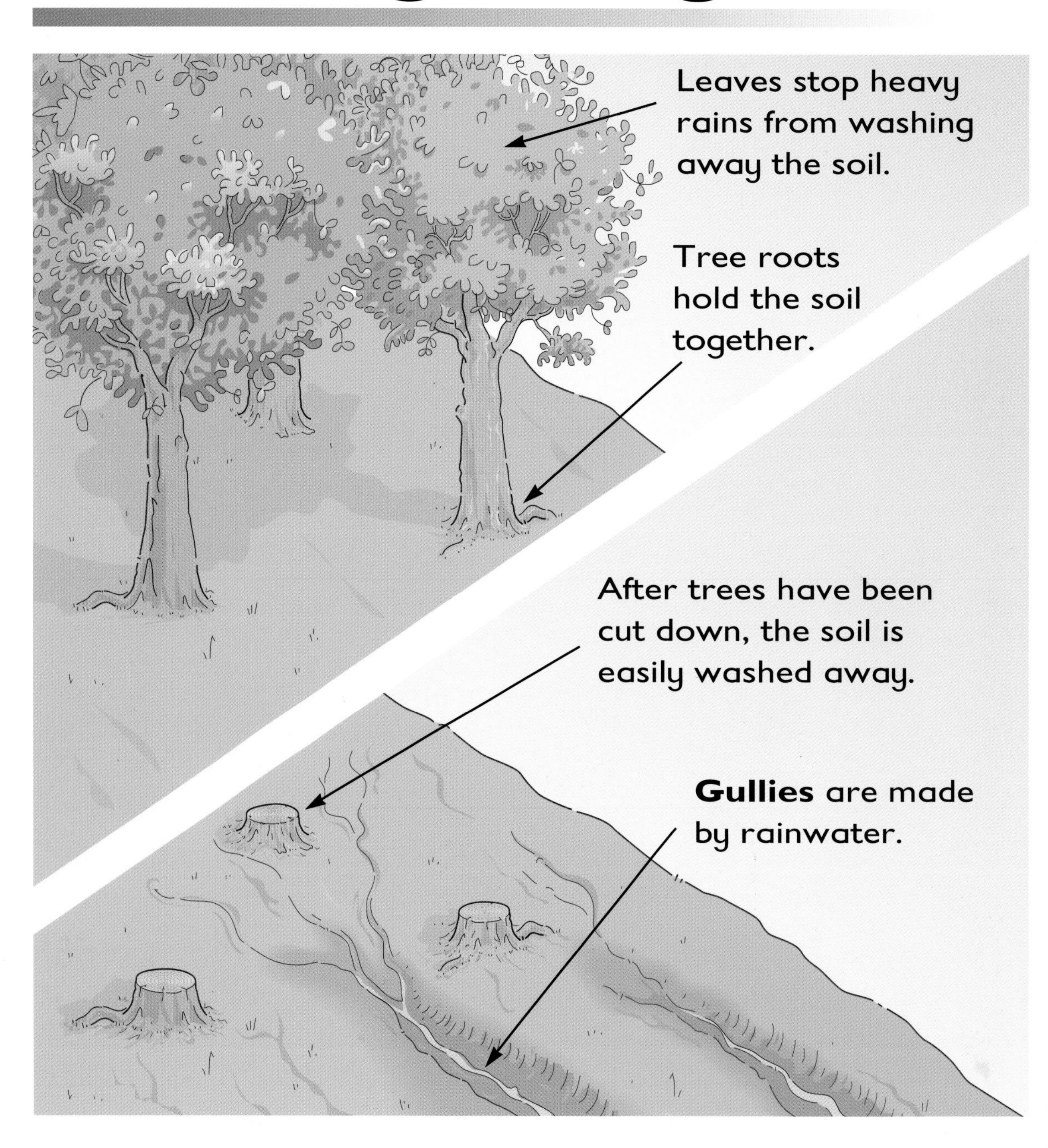

After the trees have been cut down the rain washes away the soil. The flowing water cuts gullies into the land.

Rainwater has made these gullies.

Keeping the Trees

Trees need clean air and water. Dirty air can kill trees. **Air pollution** can not always be seen. But we can see the damage it does.

Trees are killed by pollution.

planting young trees

More trees need to be planted because so many trees have been cut down. Trees take a long time to grow. It will be many years before they are full grown.

Forest Map 1

This photo of a forest was taken from an airplane. Next to the forest are two fields with bushes in between.

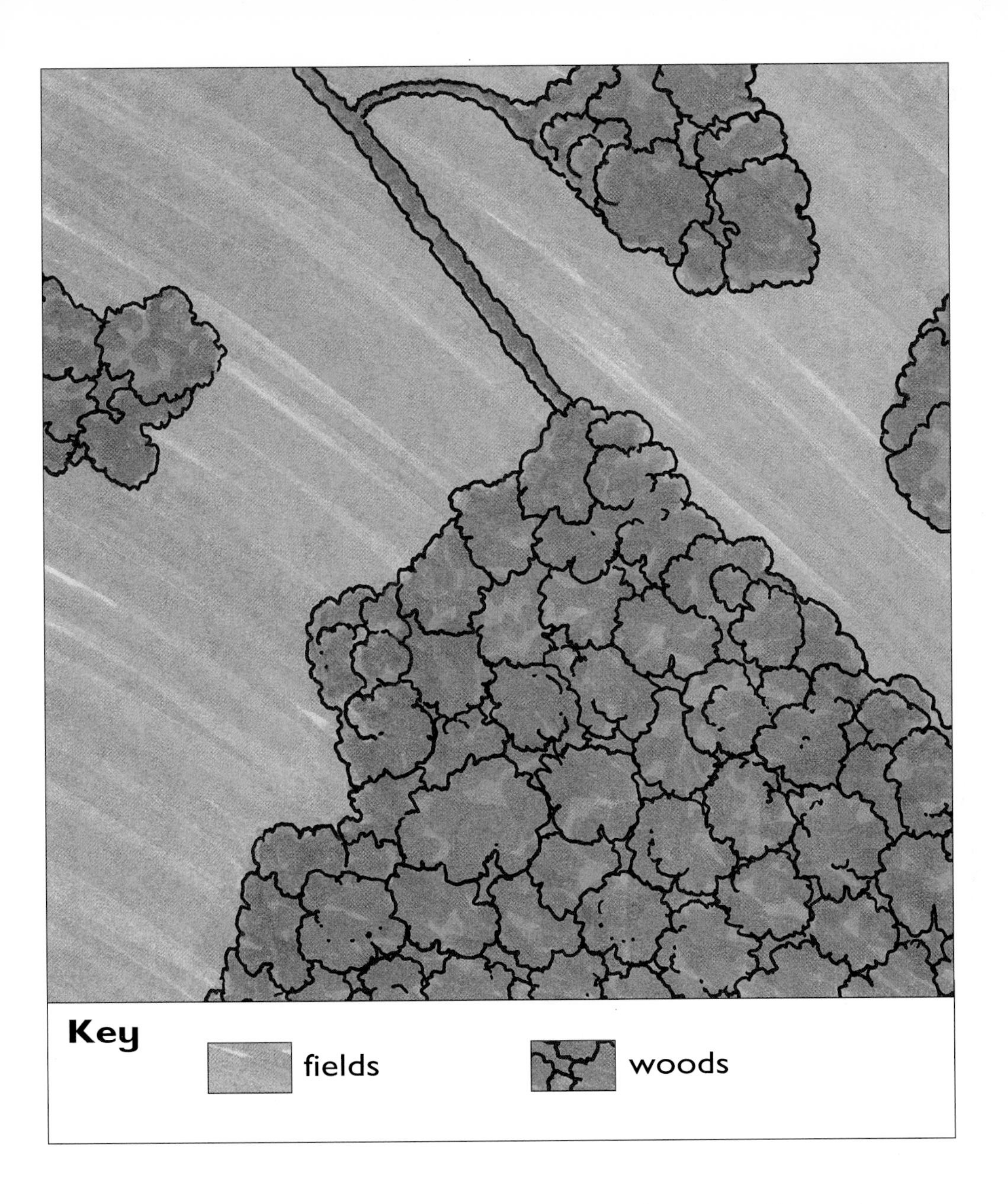

This is a map of the same place. The fields are green. The forest is shown using tree shapes.

Forest Map 2

This photo is of the same forest. The trees look smaller but you can see more of them. You can also see part of a town.

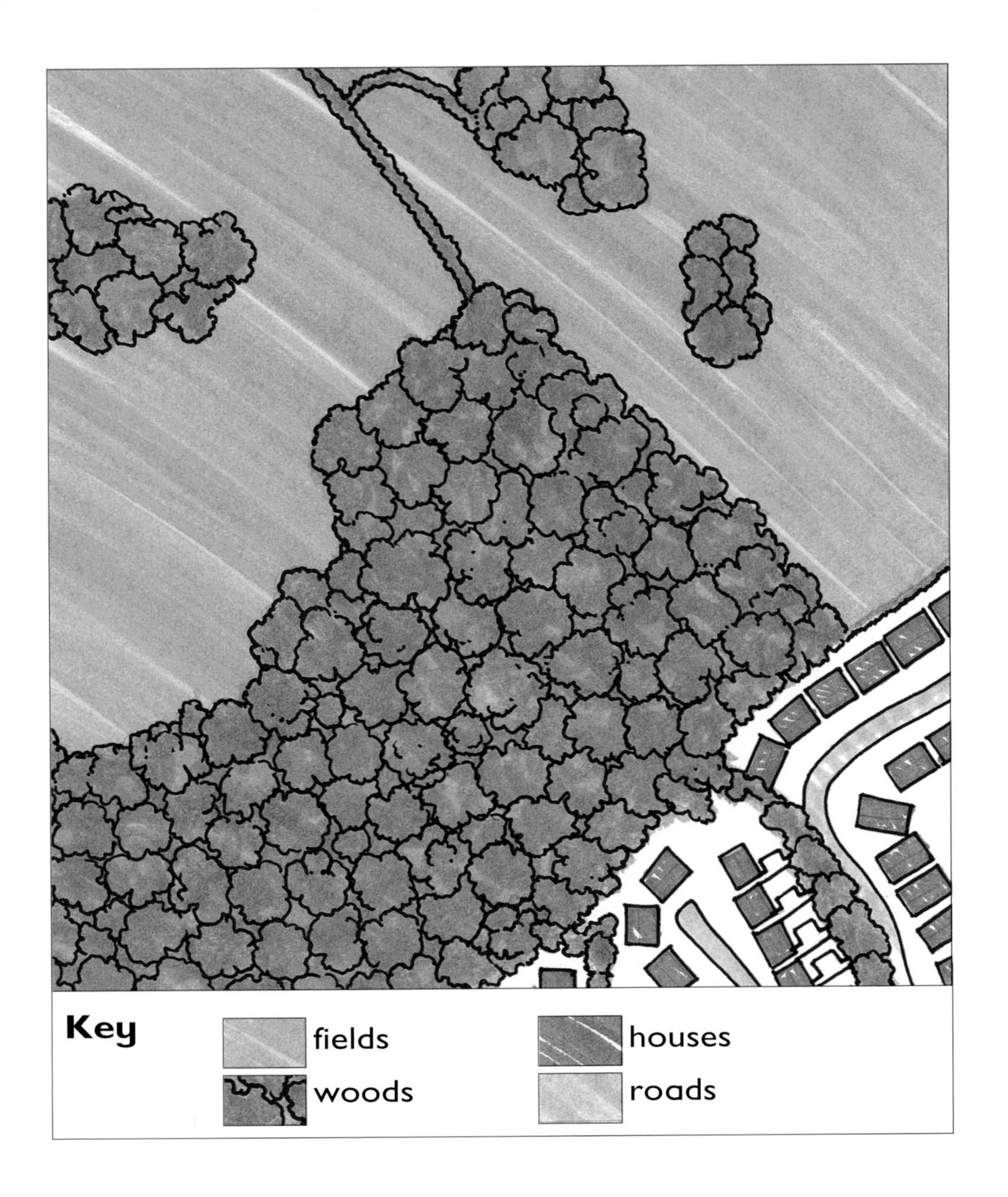

Houses and roads are shown on this map.
You can see more of the woods and fields.

Forest Map 3

You can now see all of the forest. The houses look smaller but you can see more of them. You can also see part of a main road.

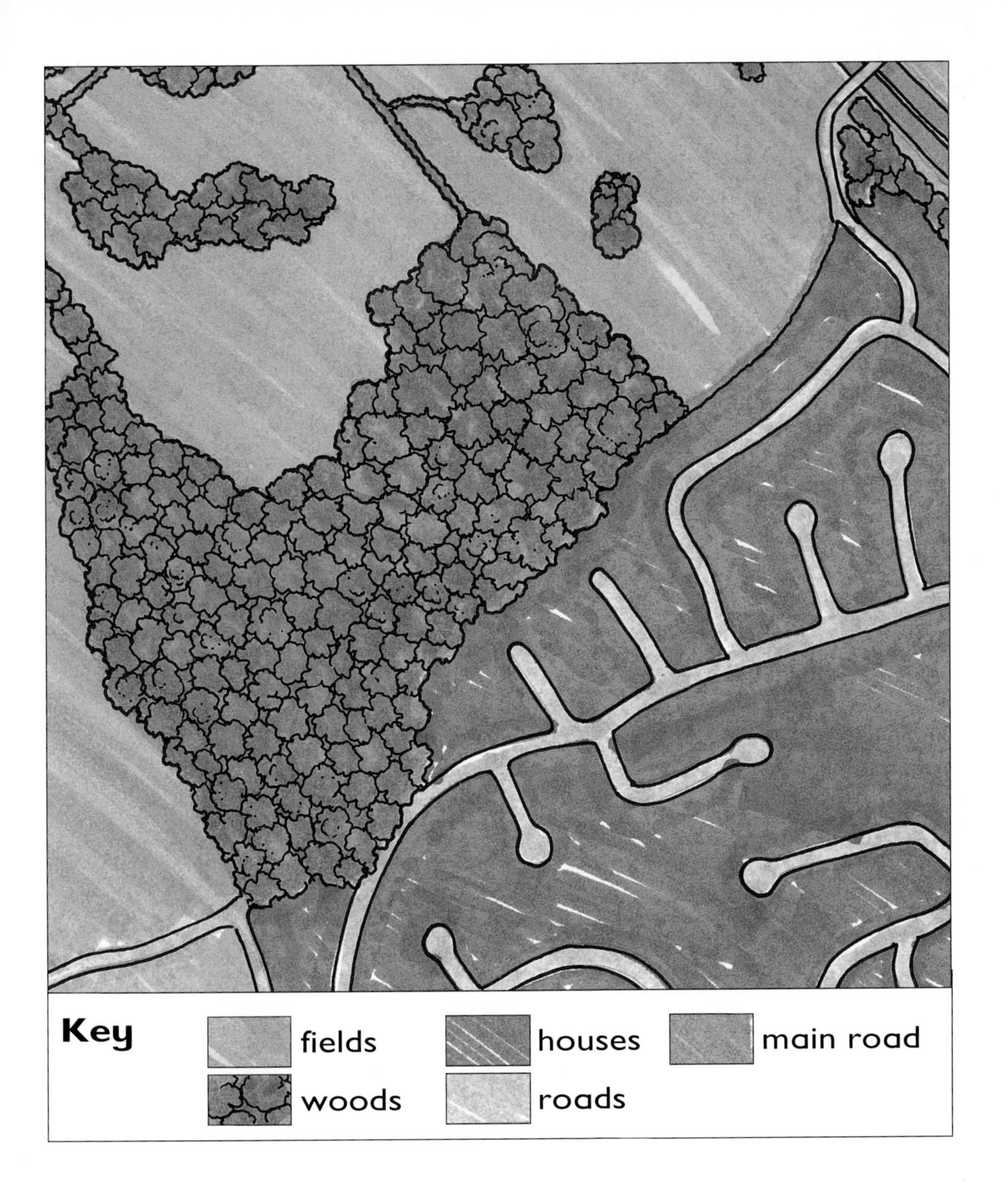

The whole forest is shown on the map. There are too many houses to show each building, so they are shown using a red color.

Amazing Forest Facts

The biggest trees in the world are giant redwoods. They grow in North America. Some of them are so big you can drive a car through them.

Tree ferns were growing when dinosaurs were alive. They still grow in some hot parts of the world.

Glossary

air pollution dirt in the air

gullies where the ground has been cut by rain water and the soil has been washed away

pine trees trees that have needles and cones

rainforests plants and trees growing together in hot, wet places

tree ferns very old type of tree that has no flowers or seeds

More Books to Read

Arnold, Caroline. *A Walk in the Woods.* Columbus, OH: Silver Press, 1990.

Bellamy, David. *Our Changing World: The Forest.* New York: Crown Books for Young Readers, 1997.

Butler, Daphne. *First Look in the Forest.* Milwaukee: Gareth Stevens, 1991.

Curran, Eileen. *Life in the Forest.* Mahwah, NJ: Troll Communications, 1985.

Greene, Carol. *Caring for Our Forests.* Springfield, NJ: Enslow Pub., 1991.

Taylor, Barbara. *Forest Life.* New York: Dorling Kindersley, 1996.

Telford, Carole and Rod Theodorou. *Amazing Journeys: Up a Rainforest Tree.* Des Plaines, IL: Heinemann Interactive Library, 1997.

Index

J 577.3
OWE
Owen, Andy,
1961-

Forests.

Wallingford Public Library
Wallingford, CT 06492
WITHDRAWN
A2170 443213 1

CHILDREN'S LIBRARY

WALLINGFORD PUBLIC LIBRARY
200 NO MAIN ST
WALLINGFORD CT 06492

BAKER & TAYLOR